Joy Cometh In The Morning

A Compilation of Inspirational Verses from
THE
HOLY BIBLE
New Testament
in the
King James Version

Gwendolyn Hall Brady

Joy Cometh in the Morning
A Compilation of Inspirational Verses from
THE
HOLY BIBLE
New Testament
in the
King James Version

Scripture quotations are from:
***THE HOLY BIBLE**, King James Version (KJV)*

Order this book online at www.trafford.com
or email orders@trafford.com

Most Trafford titles are also available at major online book retailers.

Note for Librarians: A cataloguing record for this book is available from Library and Archives Canada at www.collectionscanada.ca/amicus/index-e.html

Printed in Victoria, BC, Canada.

ISBN: 978-1-4251-9053-8 (sc)
ISBN: 978-1-4269-0164-5 (e-book)

Our mission is to efficiently provide the world's finest, most comprehensive book publishing service, enabling every author to experience success. To find out how to publish your book, your way, and have it available worldwide, visit us online at www.trafford.com

Trafford rev. 10/12/2009

Trafford PUBLISHING® www.trafford.com

North America & international
toll-free: 1 888 232 4444 (USA & Canada)
phone: 250 383 6864 ♦ fax: 812 355 4082

Joy Cometh In The Morning

A Compilation of Inspirational Verses from
THE
HOLY BIBLE
New Testament
in the
King James Version

Joy Cometh in the Morning
A Compilation of Inspirational Verses from
THE
HOLY BIBLE
New Testament
(KJV)
to:

Inspire joy and newness of life, through God's Grace, in those who feel all is hopeless. The message being that great things are possible if you only believe in God's Holy Word,

Comfort those mourning the death of a loved one,

Include in Programs for Wakes, Funeral Services and Memorial Services and

"Still" those who are fearing losses of various kinds.

REJOICE!!!

Dedicated to the beautiful memories of my parents,
Henry, Ruth and Emma Hall,
who taught me to BE STILL.

And ye now therefore have sorrow:
but I will see you again,
and your heart shall rejoice,
and your Joy no man
taketh from you!!!
-John 16:22

REJOICE!!!

In Death, there is Newness, a Celebration of Life!!

Dear God, I pray for an understanding of death
and an appreciation of life.
I pray for strength to endure and enjoy life to its
utmost, thus not fear death's coming,.
Bless me so that I will not unmercifully mourn
the loss of loved ones
but pray for their everlasting peace.
I pray to find joy and comfort in the good news:

**Verily, verily, I say unto you, That ye shall
weep and lament, but the world shall
rejoice: and ye shall be sorrowful, but your
sorrow shall be turned into joy...
And ye now therefore have sorrow: but
I will see you again, and your heart shall
rejoice, and your joy no man taketh from
you. And in that day ye shall ask me
nothing. Verily, verily, I say unto you,
Whatsoever ye shall ask the Father in my
name, he will give it you. Hitherto have ye
asked nothing in my name: ask, and ye shall
receive, that your joy may be full.**
-St. John 16: 20, 22-24

-Amen

CONTENTS
from
THE NEW TESTAMENT

But of that day and that hour knoweth no man, no, not the angels which are in heaven, neither the Son, but the Father. Take ye heed, watch and pray: for ye know not when the time is. For the Son of Man is as a man taking a far journey, who left his house, and gave authority to his servants, and to every man his work, and commanded the porter to watch. Watch ye therefore: for ye know not when the master of the house cometh, at even, or at midnight, or at the cockcrowing, or in the morning: Lest coming suddenly he find you sleeping. And what I say unto you I say unto all, Watch.

St. Mark 13: 32-37

ℰℐ

Inspiration from this Reading:
Be vigilant; watch and pray always,
as God commandeth, because no one knows
when the time will come.

But the day of the Lord will come as a thief in the night; in the which the heavens shall pass away with a great noise, and the elements shall melt with fervent heat, the earth also and the works that are therein shall be burned up. Seeing then that all these things shall be dissolved, what manner of persons ought ye to be in all holy conversation and godliness, Looking for and hasting unto the coming of the day of God, wherein the heavens being on fire shall be dissolved, and the elements shall melt with fervent heat? Nevertheless we, according to his promise, look for new heavens and a new earth, wherein dwelleth righteousness. Wherefore, beloved, seeing that ye look for such things, be diligent that ye may be found of him in peace, without spot, and blameless. And account that the longsuffering of our Lord is salvation; even as our beloved brother Paul also according to the wisdom given unto him hath written unto you; ... But grow in grace, and in the knowledge of our Lord and Savior Jesus Christ. To him be glory both now and for ever. Amen.

II Peter 3: 10-15, 18

Inspiration from this Reading:
The day of the Lord will come as a thief in the night.
Let Him find us ready.

And then shall appear the sign of the Son of man in heaven: and then shall all the tribes of the earth mourn, and they shall see the Son of man coming in the clouds of heaven with power and great glory. And he shall send his angels with a great sound of a trumpet, and they shall gather together his elect from the four winds, from one end of heaven to the other. Now learn a parable of the fig tree; When his branch is yet tender, and putteth forth leaves, ye know that summer is nigh: So likewise ye, when ye shall see all these things, know that it is near, even at the doors. Verily I say unto you, This generation shall not pass, till all these things be fulfilled. Heaven and earth shall pass away, but my words shall not pass away. But of that day and hour knoweth no man, no, not the angels of heaven, but my Father only.
St. Matthew 24: 30-36

ℰↃ

Inspiration from this Reading:
The chosen ones will be gathered from all ends of the earth. Be ready for His coming.

Whereas ye know not what shall be on the morrow. For what is your life? It is even a vapour, that appeareth for a little time, and then vanisheth away. For that ye ought to say, If the Lord will, we shall live, and do this, or that.

James 4: 14-15

Inspiration from this Reading:
None of knows what tomorrow holds. As for tomorrow and whether we will be coming or going, let us begin by saying, "If the Lord will…"

Therefore as by the offence of
one judgment came upon all men
to condemnation; even so by the
righteousness of one the free gift came
upon all men unto justification of
life. For as by one man's disobedience
many were made sinners, so by the
obedience of one shall many be made
righteous. Moreover the law entered,
that the offence might abound. But
where sin abounded, grace did much
more abound: That as sin hath reigned
unto death, even so might grace reign
through righteousness unto eternal life
by Jesus Christ our Lord.
Romans 5: 18-21

Inspiration from this Reading:
Through the free gift, eternal life by Jesus Christ our
Lord is available to us all!

...Whosoever will come after me, let him deny himself, and take up his cross, and follow me. For whosoever will save his life shall lose it; but whosoever shall lose his life for my sake and the gospel's, the same shall save it. For what shall it profit a man, if he shall gain the whole world, and lose his own soul? Or what shall a man give in exchange for his soul? Whosoever therefore shall be ashamed of me and of my words in this adulterous and sinful generation; of him also shall the Son of man be ashamed, when he cometh in the glory of his Father with the holy angels.

St. Mark 8: 34-38

Inspiration from this Reading:
If we lose our lives for Christ, we will gain eternal life!

For none of us liveth to himself, and no man dieth to himself. For whether we live, we live unto the Lord; and whether we die, we die unto the Lord: whether we live therefore, or die, we are the Lord's. For to this end Christ both died, and rose, and revived, that he might be Lord both of the dead and living. But why dost thou judge thy brother? Or why dost thou set at nought thy brother? for we shall all stand before the judgment seat of Christ. For it is written, As I Live, saith the Lord, every knee shall bow to me, and every tongue shall confess to God. So then every one of us shall give account of himself to God.
Romans 14: 7-12

Inspiration from this Reading:
All of us, the living and the dead, will have to give an account of ourselves to God!

...I am the resurrection, and the life: he that believeth in me, though he were dead, yet shall he live. And whosoever liveth and believeth in me shall never die. Believeth thou this?

St. John 11: 25-26

Inspiration from this Reading:
Those who believe in Jesus Christ will live forever!

But of the times and the seasons, brethren, ye have no need that I write unto you. For yourselves know perfectly that the day of the Lord so cometh as a thief in the night. For when they shall say, Peace and safety; then sudden destruction cometh upon them, as travail upon a woman with child; and they shall not escape. But ye, brethren, are not in darkness, that that day should overtake you as a thief. Ye are all the children of light, and the children of the day: we are not of the night, nor of darkness. Therefore let us not sleep, as do others; but let us watch and be sober...But let us, who are of the day, be sober, putting on the breastplate of faith and love; and for an helmet, the hope of salvation. For God hath not appointed us to wrath, but to obtain salvation by our Lord Jesus Christ, Who died for us, that, whether we wake or sleep, we should live together with him. Wherefore comfort yourselves together, and edify one another, even as also ye do.

I Thessalonians 5: 1-6, 8-11

Inspiration from this Reading:
Let us Pray for one another to be ready for the day when our Lord Jesus Christ comes.

And I saw a great white throne, and
him that sat on it, from whose face the
earth and the heaven fled away; and
there was found no place for them. And
I saw the dead, small and great, stand
before God; and the books were opened:
and another book was opened, which is
the book of life: and the dead were judged
out of those things which were written in
the books, according to their works. And
the sea gave up the dead which were in it;
and death and hell delivered up the dead
which were in them: and they were judged
every man according to their works. And
death and hell were cast into the lake
of fire. This is the second death. And
whosoever was not found written in the
book of life was cast into the lake of fire.

Revelation 20: 11-15

Inspiration from this Reading:
Every man, the living and the dead,
will be subject to the final judgment.

Behold, I shew you a mystery; We shall not all sleep, but we shall all be changed, In a moment, in the twinkling of an eye, at the last trump: for the trumpet shall sound, and the dead shall be raised incorruptible, and we shall be changed. For this corruptible must put on incorruption, and this mortal must put on immortality. So when this corruptible shall have put on incorruption, and this mortal shall have put on immortality, then shall be brought to pass the saying that is written, Death is swallowed up in victory. O death, where is thy sting? O grave, where is thy victory? The sting of death is sin; and the strength of sin is the law. But thanks be to God, which giveth us the victory through our Lord Jesus Christ. Therefore, my beloved brethren, be ye stedfast, unmoveable, always abounding in the work of the Lord, forasmuch as ye know that your labour is not in vain in the Lord.
I Corinthians 15: 51-58

Inspiration from this Reading:
Our work for the Lord is not in vain. We who believe know that through God, death is destroyed forever and eternal life will prevail!

For we know that if our earthly house of this tabernacle were dissolved, we have a building of God, an house not made with hands, eternal in the heavens. For in this we groan, earnestly desiring to be clothed upon with our house which is from heaven: If so be that being clothed we shall not be found naked. For we that are in this tabernacle do groan, being burdened: not for that we would be unclothed, but clothed upon, that mortality might be swallowed up of life. Now he that hath wrought us for the selfsame thing is God, who also hath given unto us the earnest of the Spirit. Therefore we are always confident, knowing that, whilst we are at home in the body, we are absent from the Lord: (For we walk by faith, not by sight:)

II Corinthians 5: 1-7

Inspiration from this Reading:
We are to walk by Faith daily, ever marching towards a home eternal in the heavens.

...Verily, verily, I say unto thee, Except a man be born again, he cannot see the kingdom of God. ...For God so loved the world, that he gave his only begotten Son, that whosoever believeth in him should not perish, but have everlasting life.

St. John 3: 3, 16

Inspiration from this Reading:
God sacrificed the life of His only Son so that those of us who believe in Jesus Christ will have everlasting life!

If ye then be risen with Christ, seek those things which are above, where Christ sitteth on the right hand of God. Set your affection on things above, not on things on the earth. For ye are dead, and your life is hid with Christ in God. When Christ, who is our life, shall appear, then shall ye also appear with him in glory...And whatsoever ye do in word or deed, do all in the name of the Lord Jesus, giving thanks to God and the Father by him.

Colossians 3: 1-4, 17

ℒ∂

Inspiration from this Reading:
If We Do Not Have Jesus Christ In Our Lives as Our Savior, We Are Dead!

Blessed be the God and Father of our Lord Jesus Christ, which according to his abundant mercy hath begotten us again unto a lively hope by the resurrection of Jesus Christ from the dead, To an inheritance incorruptible, and undefiled, and that fadeth not away, reserved in heaven for you, Who are kept by the power of God through faith unto salvation ready to be revealed in the last time.

I Peter 1: 3-5

Inspiration from this Reading:
God the Father has given us HOPE, through the resurrection of His Son Jesus Christ, to an inheritance in heaven for those who keep the Faith!

Let not your heart be troubled: ye believe in God, believe also in me. In my father's house are many mansions: if it were not so, I would have told you. I go to prepare a place for you. And if I go and prepare a place for you, I will come again, and receive you unto myself; that where I am, there ye may be also. And whither I go ye know, and the way ye know. Thomas saith unto him, Lord, we know not whither thou goest; and how can we know the way? Jesus saith unto him, I am the way, the truth, and the life; no man cometh unto the father, but by me.

St. John 14: 1-6

Inspiration from this Reading:
Do not worry about anything. God sent His Son to prepare a place for us.
Jesus Christ alone is the way to our salvation!

But we had the sentence of death in ourselves, that we should not trust in ourselves, but in God which raiseth the dead: Who delivered us from so great a death, and doth deliver: in whom we trust that he will yet deliver us;

II Corinthians 1: 9-10

Inspiration from this Reading:
God wants us to lean on Him and not depend on ourselves in any circumstance in life or death. Only trust Him for He will deliver us.

Verily, verily, I say unto you, He that heareth my word, and believeth on him that sent me, hath everlasting life, and shall not come into condemnation; but is passed from death unto life. Verily, verily, I say unto you, The hour is coming, and now is, when the dead shall hear the voice of the Son of God: and they that hear shall live.

St. John 5: 24-25

Inspiration from this Reading:
Those of us that heed His call will receive everlasting life at the appointed time!

For since by man came death, by man came also the resurrection of the dead. For as in Adam all die, even so in Christ shall all be made alive. But every man in his own order: Christ the firstfruits; afterward they that are Christ's at his coming. Then cometh the end, when he shall have delivered up the kingdom to God, even the Father; when he shall have put down all rule and all authority and power. For he must reign, till he hath put all enemies under his feet. The last enemy that shall be destroyed is death.

I Corinthians 15: 21-26

Inspiration from this Reading:

We all will die and yet we all will be raised from the dead, in the order of God because of our relationship with the risen Lord! Death has no power!

All that the Father giveth me shall come to me; and him that cometh to me I will in no wise cast out. For I came down from heaven, not to do mine own will, but the will of him that sent me. And this is the Father's will which hath sent me, that of all which he hath given me I should lose nothing, but should raise it up again at the last day. And this is the will of him that sent me, that every one which seeth the Son, and believeth on him, may have everlasting life: and I will raise him up at the last day...Verily, verily, I say unto you, He that believeth on me hath everlasting life. I am that bread of life...I am the living bread which came down from heaven: if any man eat of this bread, he shall live for ever: and the bread that I will give is my flesh, which I will give for the life of the world.

St. John 6: 37-40, 47-48, 51

Inspiration from this Reading:
Jesus Christ is the bread of life; all who believe in Him
will live forever!!

I have fought a good fight, I have finished my course, I have kept the faith: Henceforth there is laid up for me a crown of righteousness, which is the Lord, the righteous judge, shall give me at that day: and not to me only, but unto all them also that love his appearing. Do thy diligence to come shortly unto me...And the Lord shall deliver me from every evil work, and will preserve me unto his heavenly kingdom: to whom be glory for ever and ever. Amen.

II Timothy 4: 7-9, 18

Inspiration from this Reading:
The Lord crowns those who do their best, complete the course and keep the Faith!

Strive to enter in at the strait gate: for many, I say unto you, will seek to enter in, and shall not be able. When once the master of the house is risen up, and hath shut to the door, and ye begin to stand without, and to knock at the door, saying, Lord, Lord, open unto us; and he shall answer and say unto you, I know you not whence ye are: Then shall ye begin to say, We have eaten and drunk in thy presence, and thou hast taught in our streets. But he shall say, I tell you, I know you not whence ye are; depart from me, all ye workers of iniquity. There shall be weeping and gnashing of teeth, when ye shall see Abraham, and Isaac, and Jacob, and all the prophets, in the kingdom of God, and you yourselves thrust out. And they shall come from the east, and from the west, and from the north, and from the south, and shall sit down in the kingdom of God. And, behold, there are last which shall be first, and there are first which shall be last...Behold, your house is left unto you desolate: and verily I say unto you, Ye shall not see me, until the time come when ye shall say, Blessed is he that cometh in the name of the Lord.
St. Luke 13: 24-30, 35

Inspiration from this Reading:
The Kingdom of God is available only to those of us who humble ourselves in the name of the Lord.

Then said Jesus unto his disciples, If any man will come after me, let him deny himself, and take up his cross, and follow me. For whosoever will save his life shall lose it: and whosoever will lose his life for my sake shall find it. For what is a man profited, if he shall gain the whole world, and lose his own soul? Or what shall a man give in exchange for his soul? For the Son of man shall come in the glory of his Father with his angels; and then he shall reward every man according to his works. Verily I say unto you, There be some standing here, which shall not taste of death, till they see the Son of man coming in his kingdom.

St. Matthew 16: 24-28

෫ෂ

Inspiration from this Reading:
Each of us has to make our own sacrifices to the Lord to receive eternal life! Every man will be rewarded based upon his own actions.

Now faith is the substance of things hoped for, the evidence of things not seen…But without faith it is impossible to please him; for he that cometh to God must believe that he is, and that he is a rewarder of them that diligently seek him…But now they desire a better country, that is, an heavenly: wherefore God is not ashamed to be called their God: for he hath prepared for them a city.

Hebrews 11: 1, 6, 16

Inspiration from this Reading:
Like Abraham and Sarah and others who received the crown, we too have a chance to please him and die in faith!

Ask, and it shall be given you; seek, and ye shall find; knock, and it shall be opened unto you: For every one that asketh receiveth; and he that seeketh findeth; and to him that knocketh it shall be opened...
Not every one that saith unto me, Lord, Lord, shall enter into the kingdom of heaven; but he that doeth the will of my Father which is in heaven.

St. Matthew 7: 7-8, 21

Inspiration from this Reading:
If we allow God's will to be done in our lives, the
kingdom of heaven will be opened unto us!

Likewise the Spirit also helpeth our infirmities: for we know not what we should pray for as we ought: but the Spirit itself maketh intercession for us with groanings which cannot be uttered. And he that searcheth the hearts knoweth what is the mind of the Spirit, because he maketh intercession for the saints according to the will of God. And we know that all things work together for good to them that love God, to them who are the called according to his purpose.

Romans 8: 26-28

Inspiration from this Reading:
When we cannot find the words to pray,
the Spirit intercedes on our behalf and
God, who knows all, answers.

...for your Father knoweth what things ye have need of, before ye ask him. After this manner therefore pray ye: Our Father which art in heaven, Hallowed be thy name. Thy kingdom come. Thy will be done in earth, as it is in heaven. Give us this day our daily bread. And forgive us our debts, as we forgive our debtors. And lead us not into temptation, but deliver us from evil: For thine is the kingdom, and the power, and the glory, for ever. Amen.

St. Matthew 6: 8-13

Inspiration from this Reading:
Comfort is always found in praying the Lord's Prayer!

I am Alpha and Omega, the beginning and the ending, saith the Lord, which is, and which was, and which is to come, the Almighty.

Revelation 1: 8

Inspiration from this Reading:
Jesus Christ is the first and the last,
our beginning and our end!

And I saw a new heaven and a new earth: for the first heaven and the first earth were passed away; and there was no more sea. And I John saw the holy city, new Jerusalem, coming down from God out of heaven, prepared as a bride adorned for her husband. And I heard a great voice out of heaven saying, Behold, the tabernacle of God is with men, and he will dwell with them, and they shall be his people, and God himself shall be with them, and be their God... And he that sat upon the throne said, Behold, I make all things new. And he said unto me, Write: for these words are true and faithful. And he said unto me, It is done. I am Alpha and Omega, the beginning and the end. I will give unto him that is athirst of the fountain of the water of life freely. He that overcometh shall inherit all things; and I will be his God, and he shall be my son.

Revelation 21: 1-3, 5-7

ℒᴈ

Inspiration from this Reading:
It is done. We will overcome through the Grace of God. He will make all things new!

Therefore we are buried with him by baptism into death: that like as Christ was raised up from the dead by the glory of the Father, even so we also should walk in newness of life. For if we have been planted together in the likeness of his death, we shall be also in the likeness of his resurrection:...
For he that is dead is freed from sin. Now if we be dead with Christ, we believe that we shall also live with him: Knowing that Christ being raised from the dead dieth no more; death hath no more dominion over him.

Romans 6: 4-5, 7-9

Inspiration from this Reading:
Through Faith in Jesus Christ, in Death, let us Celebrate a Newness of Life!!

...Be thou faithful unto death, and I will give thee a crown of life.

Revelation 2: 10

ℒ𝒶

Inspiration from this Reading:
The greatest reward for our faithfulness
unto death is eternal life!

But is now made manifest
by the appearing of our
Savior Jesus Christ, who
hath abolished death,
and hath brought life
and immortality to light
through the gospel.
II Timothy 1: 10

Inspiration from this Reading:
Spread the Good News! Our Savior Jesus Christ is our
Life and our Light!

Who shall separate us from the love of Christ? shall tribulation, or distress, or persecution, or famine, or nakedness, or peril, or sword? As it is written, For thy sake we are killed all the day long; we are accounted as sheep for the slaughter. Nay, in all these things we are more than conquerors through him that loved us. For I am persuaded, that neither death, nor life, nor angels, nor principalities, nor powers, nor things present, nor things to come, Nor height, nor depth, nor any other creature, shall be able to separate us from the love of God, which is in Christ Jesus our Lord.

Romans 8: 35-39

Inspiration from this Reading:
Nothing, including death, can separate us from the love of God, which is in Christ Jesus our Lord!

...Blessed are the dead which die in the Lord from henceforth: Yea, saith the Spirit, that they may rest from their labours; and their works do follow them.
Revelation 14: 13

Inspiration from this Reading:
Those that die in the Lord are resting in Peace.

But I would not have you to be ignorant, brethren, concerning them which are asleep, that ye sorrow not, even as others which have no hope. For if we believe that Jesus died and rose again, even so them also which sleep in Jesus will God bring with him. For this we say unto you by the word of the Lord, that we which are alive and remain unto the coming of the Lord shall not prevent them which are asleep. For the Lord himself shall descend from heaven with a shout, with the voice of the archangel, and with the trump of God: and the dead in Christ shall rise first: Then we which are alive and remain shall be caught up together with them in the clouds, to meet the Lord in the air: and so shall we ever be with the Lord. Wherefore comfort one another with these words.

I Thessalonians 4: 13-18

Inspiration from this Reading:
Comfort those who mourn for them that are dead in Christ. Tell the mourners that in the Lord's second coming, the dead in Christ will rise first and those of us who believe in Jesus will also have eternal rest with the Lord!

Blessed are they that mourn: for they shall be comforted.
St. Matthew 5: 4

୫ଦ

Inspiration from this Reading:
True happiness comes when we believe in the Word of the Lord. For even when we mourn in times of sorrow, we know in our hearts that the Lord will Bless and Comfort us!

And whatsoever ye shall ask in my name, that will I do, that the Father may be glorified in the Son. If ye shall ask any thing in my name, I will do it. If ye love me, keep my commandments. And I will pray the Father, and he shall give you another Comforter, that he may abide with you for ever; Even the Spirit of truth; whom the world cannot receive, because it seeth him not, neither knoweth him: but ye know him; for he dwelleth with you, and shall be in you. I will not leave you comfortless: I will come to you. Yet a little while, and the world seeth me no more; but ye see me: because I live, ye shall live also. At that day ye shall know that I am in my Father, and ye in me, and I in you...But the Comforter, which is the Holy Ghost, whom the Father will send in my name, he shall teach you all things, and bring all things to your remembrance, whatsoever I have said unto you. Peace I leave with you, my peace I give unto you: not as the world giveth, give I unto you. Let not your heart be troubled, neither let it be afraid.
St. John 14: 13-20, 26-27

Inspiration from this Reading:
No matter what the situation, He will not leave us comfortless! Just call on Him and the Comforter will come!

...Seek ye first the kingdom of God, and his righteousness; and all these things shall be added unto you. Take therefore no thought for the morrow: for the morrow shall take thought for the things of itself. Sufficient unto the day is the evil thereof.

St. Matthew 6: 33-34

Inspiration from this Reading:
If we keep the faith and serve God only, we would have no need to worry about anything in this life!

Come unto me, all ye that labour and are heavy laden, and I will give you rest. Take my yoke upon you, and learn of me; for I am meek and lowly in heart: and ye shall find rest upon your souls. For my yoke is easy, and my burden is light.

St. Matthew 11: 28-30

Inspiration from this Reading:
God wants us to bring our heavy burdens to Him in Prayer.
He will give rest to the weary!

I can do all things through Christ which strengtheneth me.
Philippians 4:13

Inspiration from this Reading:
Jesus Christ alone is the source of our strength in all things and at all times in our lives!!

Blessed be God, even the Father of our Lord Jesus Christ, the Father of mercies, and the God of all comfort; Who comforteth us in all our tribulation, that we may be able to comfort them which are in any trouble, by the comfort wherewith we ourselves are comforted of God. For as the sufferings of Christ abound in us, so our consolation also aboundeth by Christ. And whether we be afflicted, it is for your consolation and salvation, which is effectual in the enduring of the same sufferings which we also suffer: or whether we be comforted, it is for your consolation and salvation. And our hope of you is stedfast, knowing, that as ye are partakers of the sufferings, so shall ye be also of the consolation. For we would not, brethren, have you ignorant of our trouble which came to us in Asia, that we were pressed out of measure, above strength, insomuch that we despaired even of life: But we had the sentence of death in ourselves, that we should not trust in ourselves, but in God which raiseth the dead: Who delivered us from so great a death, and doth deliver: in whom we trust that he will yet deliver us; Ye also helping together by prayer for us, that for the gift bestowed upon us by the means of many persons thanks may be given by many on our behalf.

II Corinthians 1: 3-11

Inspiration from this Reading:
God comforts us in our trials and tribulations. We should use the help He gives us to provide consolation to others who are in trouble, thus, we will be doing the works of the Lord!!!

Rejoice with them that do rejoice, and weep with them that weep.
Romans 12: 15

Inspiration from this Reading:
Ask God for strength to be glad with those who are joyful and to mourn with those who are mourning.

...the members should have the same care one for another. And whether one member suffer, all the members suffer with it; or one member be honoured, all the members rejoice with it.

I Corinthians 12: 25-26

℘❧

Inspiration from this Reading:
We are all members of the body of Christ...when one suffers we all suffer, when one rejoices we all rejoice.

Bear ye one another's burdens, and so fulfil the law of Christ...
As we have the opportunity, let us do good unto all men, especially unto them who are of the household of faith.

Galatians 6: 2, 10

Inspiration from this Reading:
Christ asks that we, as Christians, bear one another's burdens.

There hath no temptation taken you but such as is common to man: but God is faithful, who will not suffer you to be tempted above that ye are able; but will with the temptation also make a way to escape, that ye may be able to bear it.

I Corinthians 10: 13

❧

Inspiration from this Reading:
God will not permit us to suffer more than we can bear! Through it all, He will provide a way out!

Not as though I had already attained, either were already perfect: but I follow after, if that I may apprehend that for which also I am apprehended of Christ Jesus. Brethren, I count not myself to have apprehended: but this one thing I do, forgetting those things which are behind, and reaching forth unto those things which are before, I press toward the mark for the prize of the high calling of God in Christ Jesus. Let us therefore, as many as be perfect, be thus minded: and if in any thing ye be otherwise minded, God shall reveal even this unto you. Nevertheless, whereto we have already attained, let us walk by the same rule, let us mind the same thing.

Philippians 3: 12-16

Inspiration from this Reading:
Let us pray to forget those things behind us and press toward the prize ahead that is available only through Christ Jesus.

...For he hath said, I will never leave thee, nor forsake thee. So that we may boldly say, The Lord is my helper, and I will not fear what man shall do unto me...Jesus Christ the same yesterday, and to-day, and for ever...Now the God of peace, that brought again from the dead our Lord Jesus, that great shepherd of the sheep, through the blood of the everlasting covenant, Make you perfect in every good work to do his will, working in you that which is well-pleasing in his sight, through Jesus Christ; to whom be glory for ever and ever. Amen.

Hebrews 13: 5-6, 8, 20-21

Inspiration from this Reading:
Jesus Christ never changes in His love for us. He is the same yesterday, today and forever!

*...and, lo, I am with you alway,
even unto the end of the world.
Amen.*
St. Matthew 28: 20

ℰ∂

Inspiration from this Reading:
Fear not, for we are never alone.
Jesus Christ is always there!

Be careful for nothing; but in every thing by prayer and supplication with thanksgiving let your request be made known unto God And the peace of God, which passeth all understanding, shall keep your hearts and minds through Christ Jesus...Not that I speak in respect of want: for I have learned, in whatsoever state I am, therewith to be content. I know both how to be abased, and I know how to abound: every where and in all things I am instructed both to be full and to be hungry, both to abound and to suffer need...But my God shall supply all your need according to his riches in glory by Christ Jesus.

Philippians 4: 6-7, 11-12, 19

℘∂

Inspiration from this Reading:
Let us submit our Prayer Requests to Christ Jesus. Then, stand fast on Faith in times of need and in times of prosperity!

Even so faith, if it hath not works, is dead, being alone. Yea, a man may say, Thou hast faith, and I have works: shew me thy faith without thy works, and I will shew thee my faith by my works…Ye see then how that by works a man is justified, and not by faith only…For as the body without the spirit is dead, so faith without works is dead also.

James 2: 17-18, 24, 26

Inspiration from this Reading:

We are to demonstrate our faith through our actions for Faith without works is dead! When we mourn, we should believe and act through our Faith that Christ will comfort us and He will!

Looking unto Jesus the author and finisher of our faith; who for the joy that was set before him endured the cross, despising the shame, and is set down at the right hand of the throne of God. For consider him that endured such contradiction of sinners against himself, lest ye be wearied and faint in your minds. Ye have not yet resisted unto blood, striving against sin ...Wherefore we receiving a kingdom which cannot be moved, let us have grace, whereby we may serve God acceptably with reverence and godly fear: For our God is a consuming fire.

Hebrews 12: 2-4, 28-29

Inspiration from this Reading:
Be grateful, for nothing we will endure equals Christ's suffering on the cross so that we may have eternal life!

Verily, verily, I say unto you, That ye shall weep and lament, but the world shall rejoice: and ye shall be sorrowful, but your sorrow shall be turned into joy...

And ye now therefore have sorrow: but I will see you again, and your heart shall rejoice, and your joy no man taketh from you. And in that day ye shall ask me nothing. Verily, verily, I say unto you, Whatsoever ye shall ask the Father in my name, he will give it you. Hitherto have ye asked nothing in my name: ask, and ye shall receive, that your joy may be full.

St. John 16: 20, 22-24

Inspiration from this Reading:
Ask it in His Name, and He will turn sorrow into joy!

And God shall wipe away
all tears from their eyes; and
there shall be no more death,
neither sorrow, nor crying,
neither shall there be any
more pain: for the former
things are passed away.
Revelation 21: 4

Inspiration from this Reading:
When the change comes, we will be rewarded…
there will be no more death, grief or pain,
only Joy on the Lord's day!

WE WILL REJOICE!

Whether we have sorrow from the death of a loved one or a terminal illness, from the loss of a job or worry in the midst of a storm, we should be still and know that God will deliver us through it all!

God is in control of our lives. He is our Alpha and our Omega, our beginning and our ending. Gwendolyn Hall Brady, a former Sunday School Teacher, has prepared two editions of "***Joy Cometh in the Morning***," one compilation of selected inspirational scripture from the Old Testament and one from the New Testament of **The Holy Bible** in the King James version. Each edition helps us to understand death and eternal life. Moreover, each contains His words of comfort and guidance on how to be still in the midst of a storm.

ℰᶟ